Animal Babies

by Chris Michaels

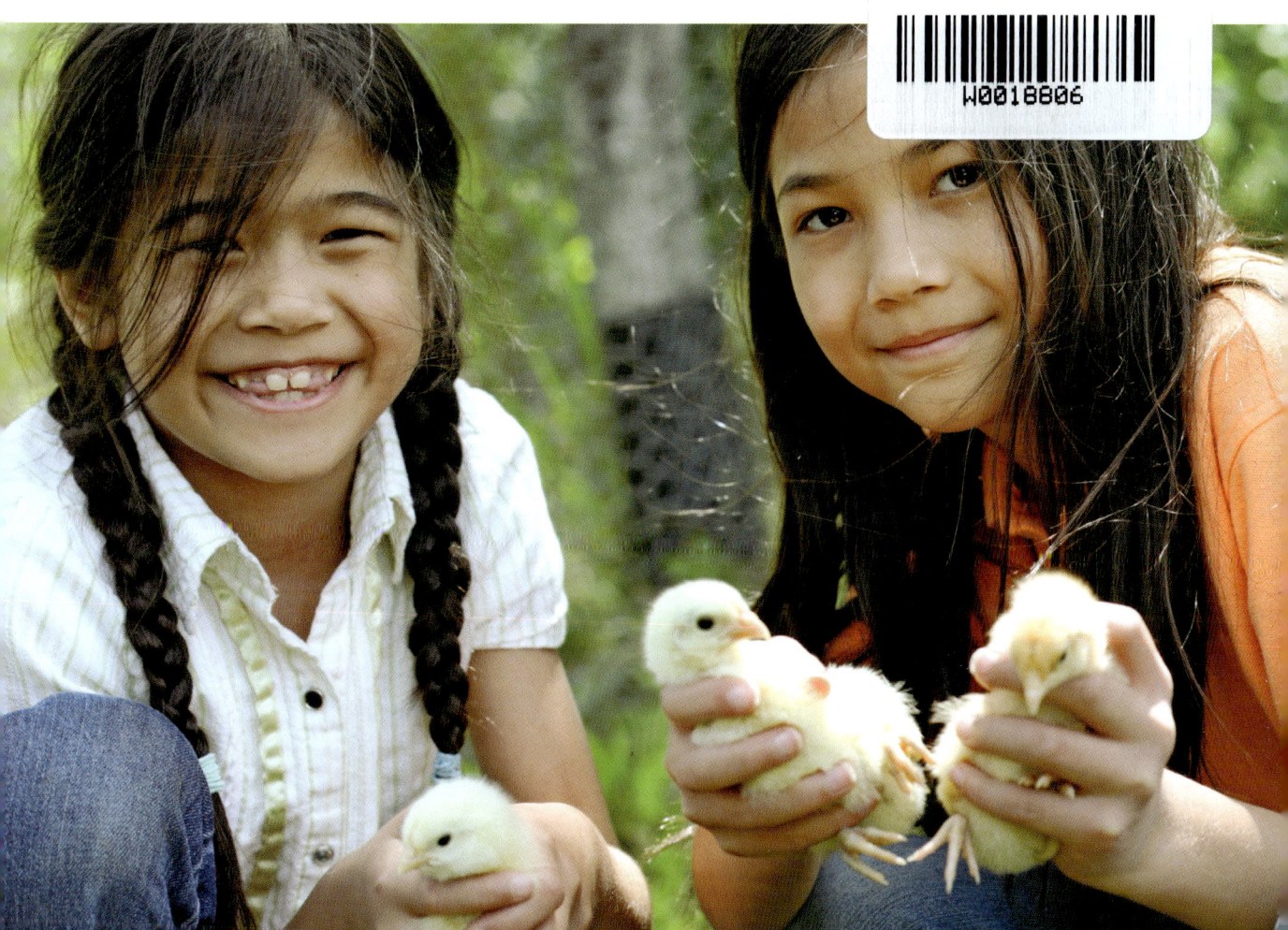

Picture Words

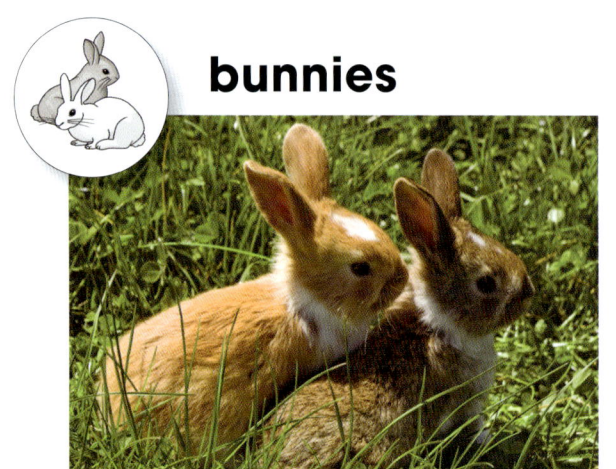
bunnies

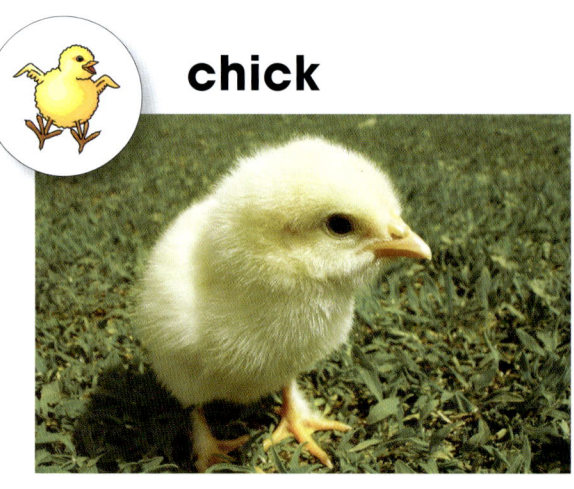
chick

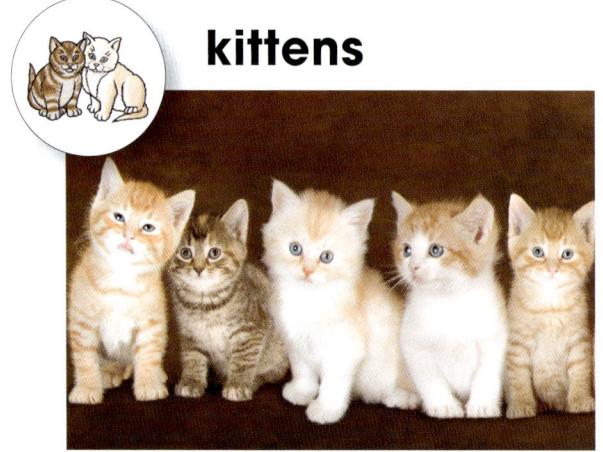
kittens

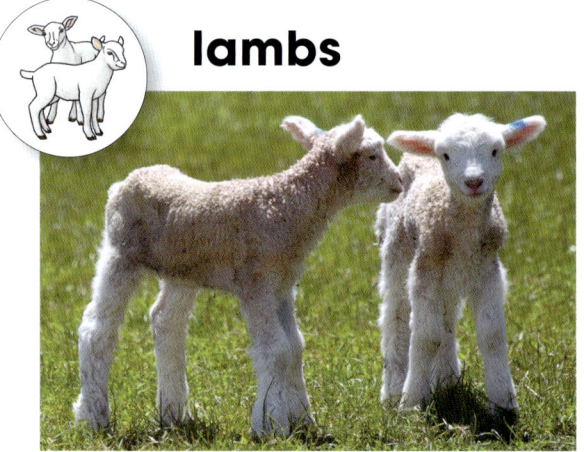
lambs

2

puppies

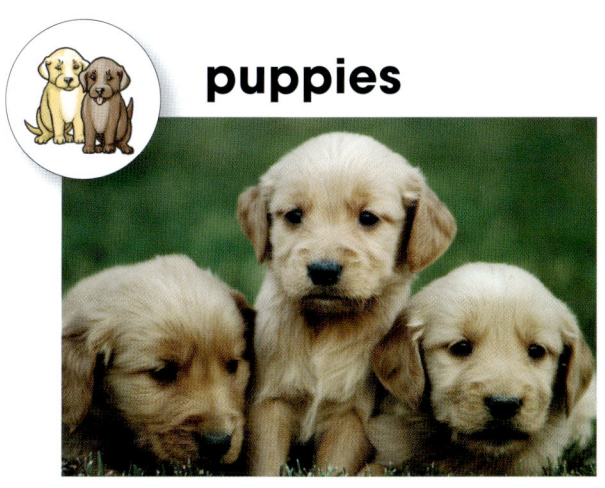

I

play

with

I play with 1 .

chick

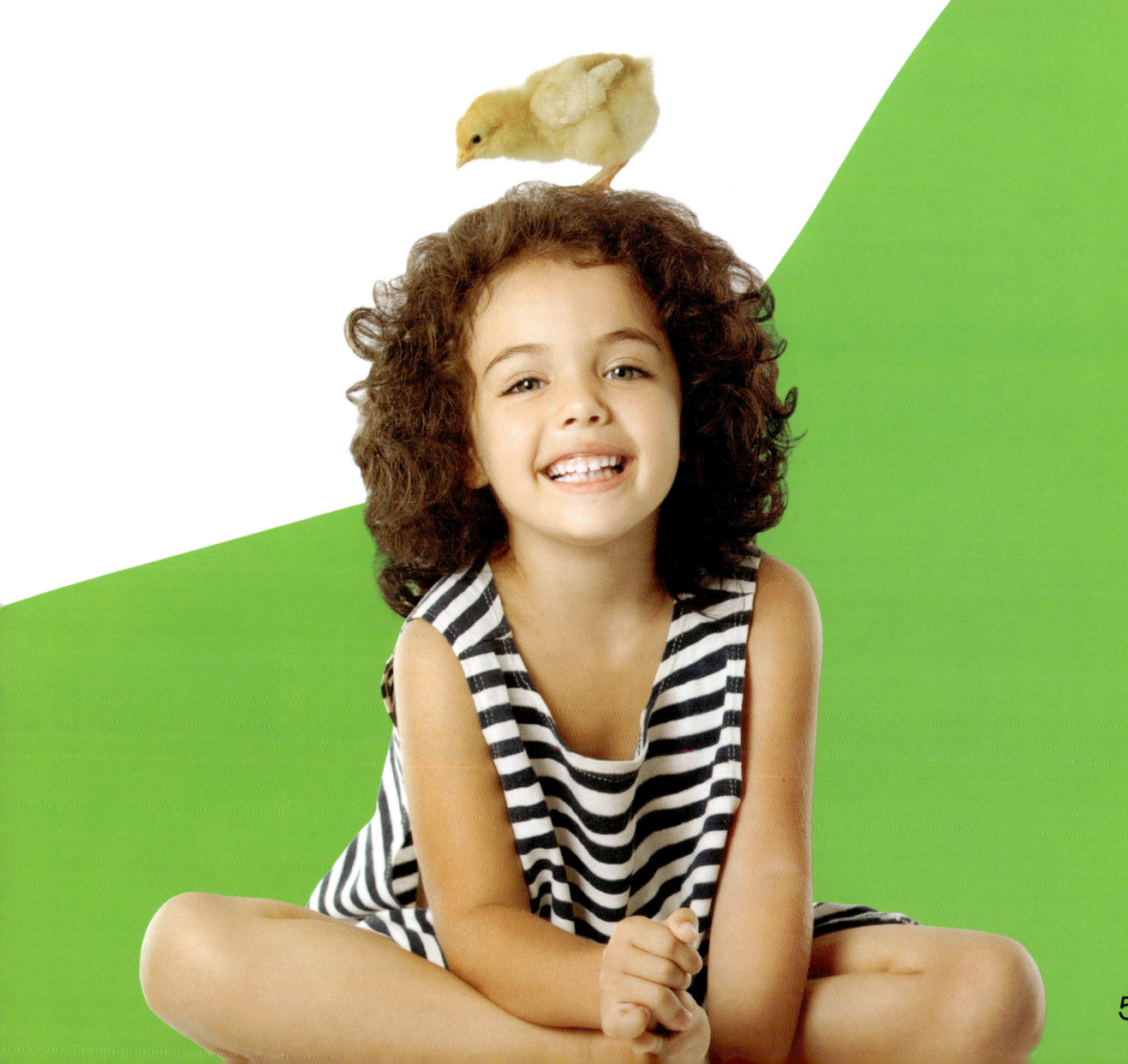

I play with 2 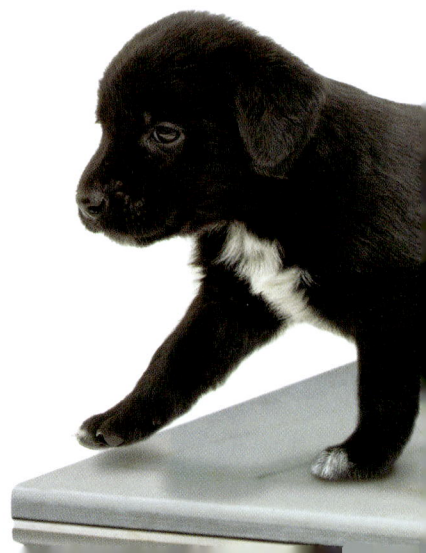 .

puppies

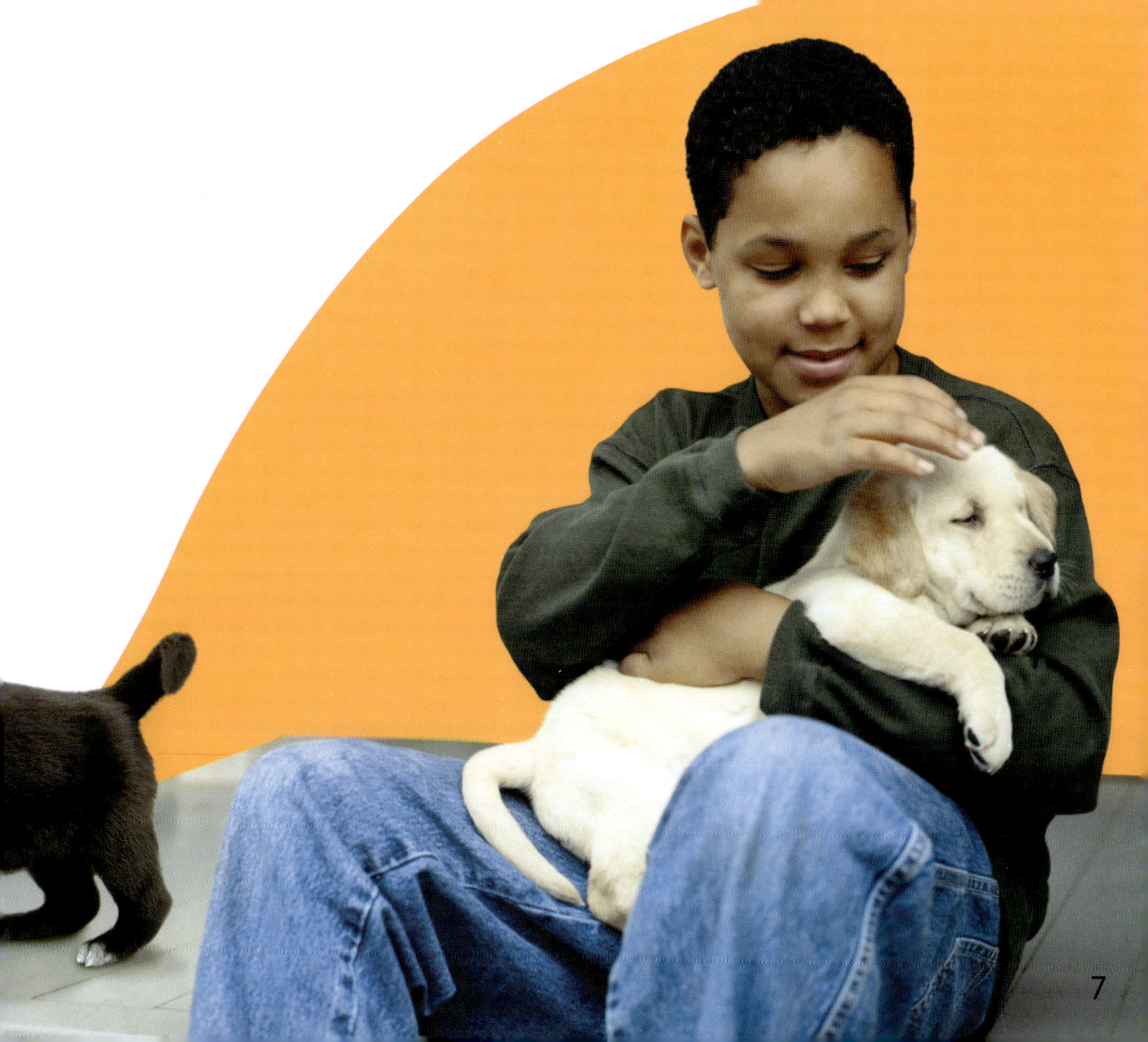

I play with 3 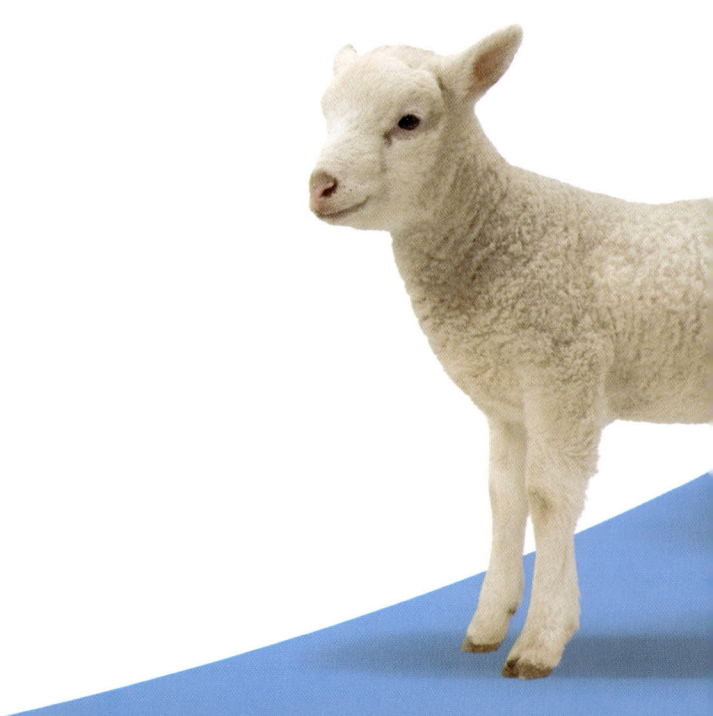.

lambs

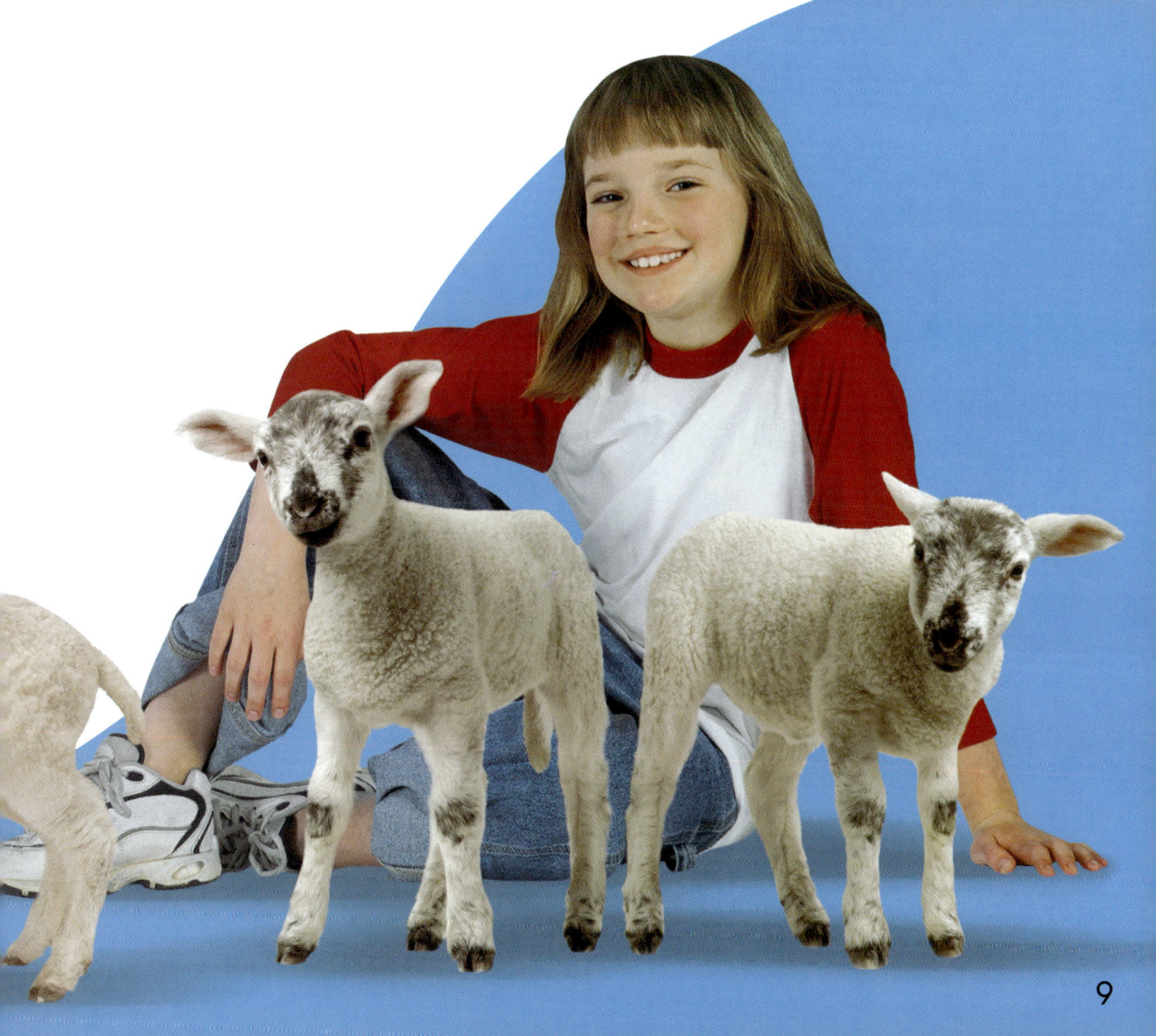

I play with 4 .

bunnies

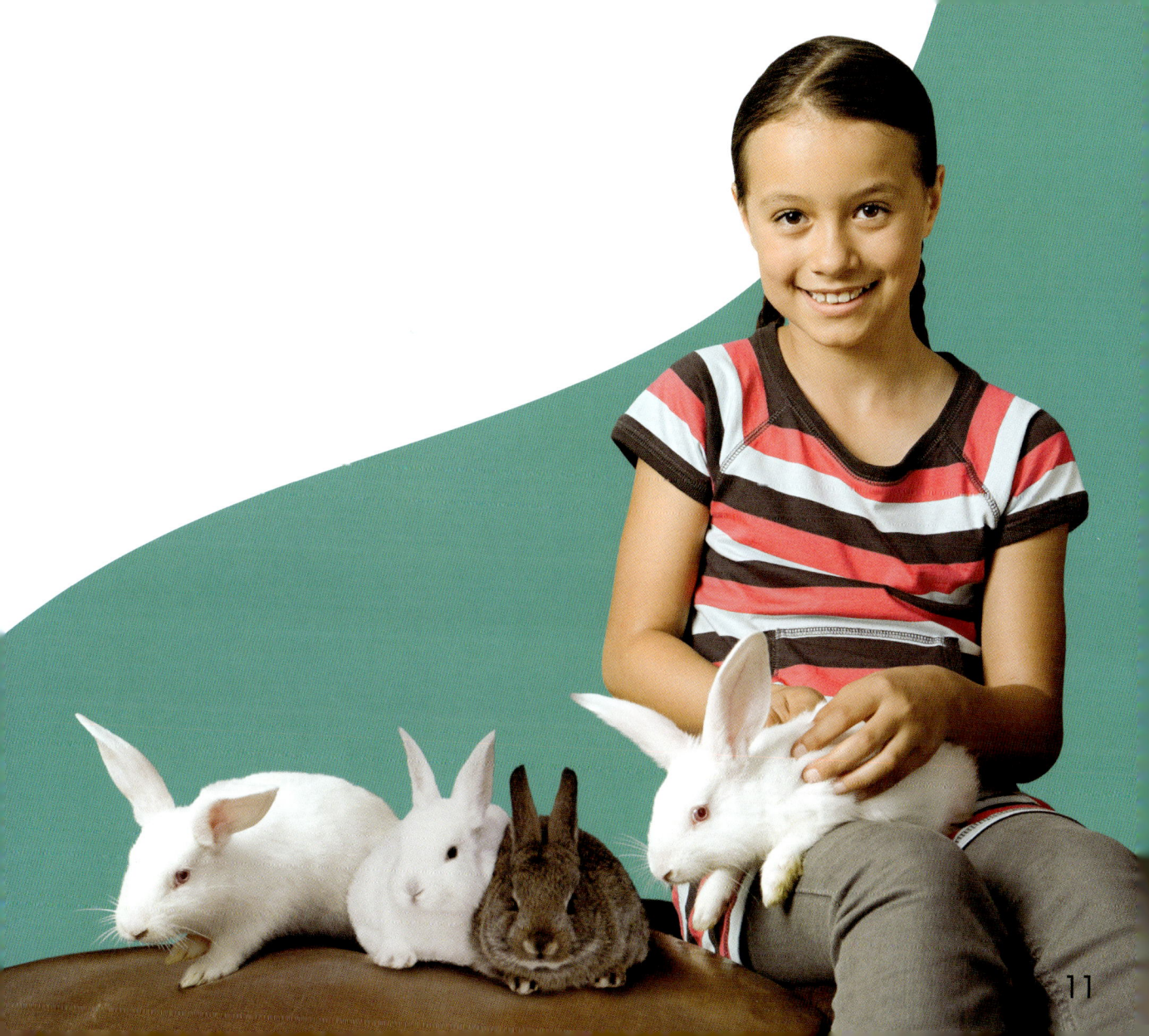

I play with 5 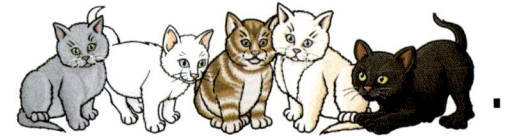.

kittens

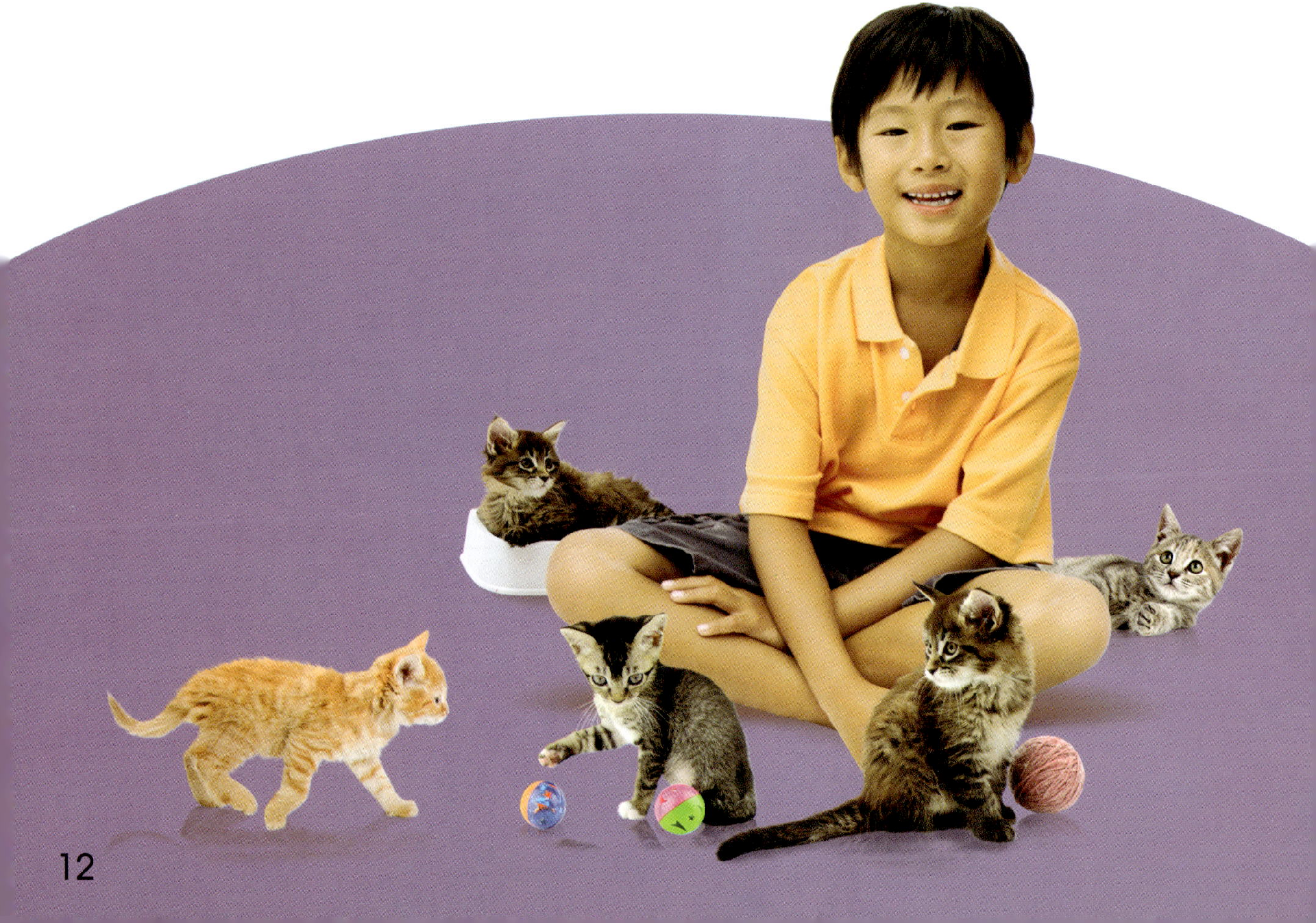